My Pet Rabbit

written by Kelly Gaffney

photography by Ned Meldrum

Look at the rabbits.

The rabbits are grey.

Rabbits are good pets to have.

The rabbits are not very big.
This girl can fit a rabbit
in her hands.

The rabbits have big ears and brown eyes.
They have little tails, too.

ears

eye

tail

Rabbits can get very hungry.

They eat green grass.

They eat little bits of carrot.

The rabbits have water, too.

Look at this rabbit.
It is sitting with the girl.

Look at this rabbit.
It is sitting
in the green grass.

Rabbits are fun to play with.
You can play with rabbits
in the garden.
The rabbits can jump and hop
in the green grass.

The rabbits hide in the green grass.

They hide inside pots, too!

This girl is looking for her rabbits.

15

Look!

Can you see the little grey rabbits?